Health and My Body

Know Your Senses

by Mari Schuh

T0084494

PEBBLE
a capstone imprint

Pebble Explore is published by Pebble, an imprint of Capstone
1710 Roe Crest Drive
North Mankato, Minnesota 56003
www.capstonepub.com

**Library of Congress Cataloging-in-Publication Data is available on
the Library of Congress website.**
ISBN: 978-1-9771-2390-9 (library binding)
ISBN: 978-1-9771-2690-0 (paperback)
ISBN: 978-1-9771-2427-2 (ebook PDF)

Summary: Your five senses help make every day complete. Learn
about the importance of taste, touch, sight, smell, and hearing.

Image Credits
Shutterstock: 1234zoom, 19, AJP, 15, AlexandrMusuc, 13, Ann in the
uk, 24, Cherry-Merry, 10, cynoclub, 14, Expensive, 5, feelartfeelant, 8,
GUNDAM_Ai, 29, GWImages, 21, kokanphoto, 12, Monkey Business
Images, 27, New Africa, 28, OSSIBUS, 23, Photo Spirit, 17, photonova,
design element, Rob Hainer, Cover, Samuel Borges Photography, 4,
solar22, 20, StockImageFactory.com, 11, VaLiza, 7, VectorMine, 16,
wavebreakmedia, 6, 26

Editorial Credits
Editor: Christianne Jones; Designer: Sarah Bennett; Media Researcher:
Morgan Walters; Production Specialist: Laura Manthe

All internet sites appearing in back matter were available and
accurate when this book was sent to press.

Table of Contents

Bold words are in the glossary.

Your Senses

Look around you. What things do you see? What things can you touch? Your senses help you learn about the world around you.

You have five main senses. They are smelling, tasting, hearing, seeing, and touching. You have five main sense organs. They are your nose, tongue, ears, eyes, and skin.

How do your senses work? Many parts work together. **Nerves** carry messages to your brain. They tell your brain about things around you.

Smelling

Take a deep breath. What do you smell? You can smell thousands of scents! Pizza and popcorn smell good. Garbage smells bad. Some things have a strong scent. Smell some cookies. They smell yummy!

Your sense of smell keeps you safe. Old milk smells stinky. Yuck! The bad smell tells you it's not safe to drink. Smelling smoke tells you fire is nearby.

Your nose and brain work together to smell. Scents float in the air. Scents go into your nose when you breathe in air. The scents hit nerve cells in your nose. Those cells send messages to your brain. Then your brain lets you know what you're smelling.

Smelling also helps you taste! Your sense of smell and sense of taste work as a team. Scents from food help you taste better.

Tasting

What did you eat today? Did you eat an apple? A piece of cake? Maybe you enjoyed some yogurt. You use your tongue to taste food. Look! Small bumps cover your tongue. Inside those bumps are tiny taste buds. Your mouth and throat have taste buds too.

Food mixes with saliva in your mouth. Parts of the food go into your taste buds. Taste buds help send signals to your brain. Then you know the taste of your food. There are five main tastes. They are sweet, salty, sour, bitter, and **umami**.

Most cookies and treats are sweet. Chips and nuts can taste salty. A lemon is sour. Pickles are also sour. Coffee tastes bitter. Some chocolate is bitter too. Take a bite of cheese. Umami is a taste found in meat and cheese.

Hearing

You hear many sounds all day. Beep! Beep! An alarm clock wakes you up. Your phone rings. It's your friend. He wants to play. Ruff! Ruff! A dog barks. You're using your sense of hearing.

Listen carefully. Some sounds are quiet. A clock ticks. Rain gently falls. A friend whispers. Sounds can also be very loud. A horn blows. The crowd cheers. A baby cries. Loud sounds are easier to hear.

Sound moves in waves. You hear the waves, but you can't see them. First, they go into your ear. The waves hit your **eardrum**. It **vibrates**.

Many parts in your ear work together. The **cochlea** is a snail-shaped part of the ear. It helps send sound messages to the brain.

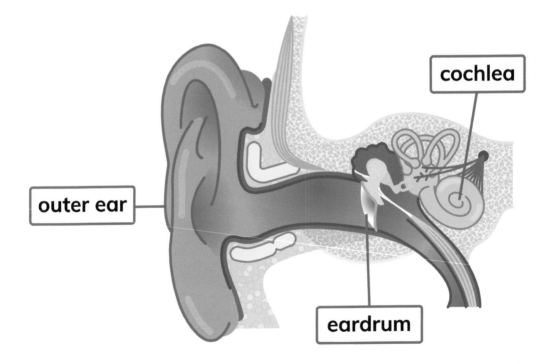

cochlea

outer ear

eardrum

Loud sounds can keep people safe.
A siren blares! A fire truck is on the way
to a fire. Tweet! Tweet! A whistle blows.
Now it is safe to cross the street.

Seeing

You see with your eyes. When you read, you use your sense of sight. Your eyes let you see words and pictures on the page. Red, yellow, blue! Circles and squares! You see shapes and colors.

Your eyes let you see things very close to you. You can see dirt on your hands. Your eyes also let you see things far away. You can see fireworks in the sky. What do you see around you now?

How do you see? First, light bounces off objects. Then the light goes into your eyes. A lens in your eye bends the light. The light hits your **retina**. It has cells called rods and cones. Rods see shapes. Cones see colors. They help send signals to your brain. Your brain lets you know what you see!

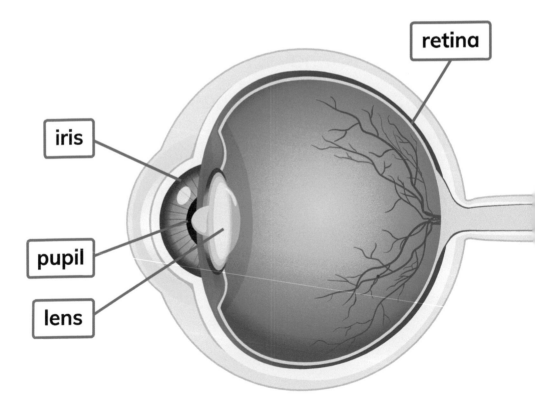

retina

iris

pupil

lens

The dark circle in your eye is the pupil. It lets in light. Your pupils change size. They get bigger when it's dark. This helps them let in more light. The colored part of your eye is the iris.

Touching

Grab a towel. How does it feel? Is it rough or soft? Is it wet or dry? Your sense of touch tells you many things. It tells you if water is warm or cold. You find out if a rock is sharp or smooth.

Your sense of touch also helps keep you safe. A cactus is prickly. Ouch! A stove is hot. Scissors are sharp. Your skin senses pain. Pain keeps you away from things that hurt. You move away quickly!

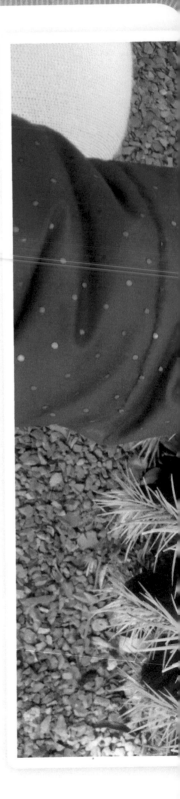

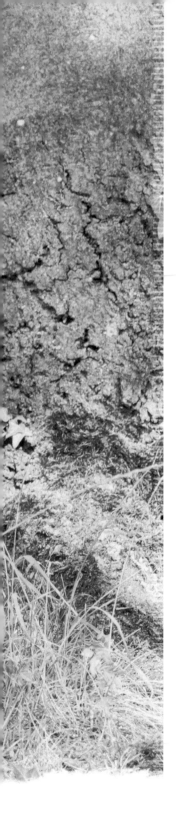

Your sense of touch comes from your skin. Your skin has tiny sensors. The sensors help send messages to your brain. Your brain tells you how something feels. An ice cube feels cold. A feather feels soft.

Some parts of your body have a very good sense of touch. These parts have lots of sensors. Fingers, toes, lips, and your tongue can sense touch well.

Problems with Senses

People can have problems with their senses. When people have problems with one sense, they use their other senses more. They can still learn about the world around them.

Some people need help seeing. They wear glasses or contacts. Some people are blind. They can use **braille** to read.

People who can't hear very well might use hearing aids. Some people can't hear at all. They are deaf. They use **sign language** to communicate. They might use a **cochlear implant** to help them hear too.

Look around you again. Think about your five senses. Your senses help you play. They help you read books and enjoy tasty food. Now use your senses to enjoy the world around you.

Glossary

braille (BRAYL)—a set of raised dots that stand for letters and numbers

cochlea (KOH-klee-uh)—a spiral-shaped part of the ear that helps send sound messages to the brain

cochlear implant (KOK-lee-uhr im-PLANT)—a device that helps someone hear better by sending sounds directly to the brain

eardrum (IHR-druhm)—a thin layer of tissue between the outer and middle parts of the ear

nerve (NURV)—a thin fiber that sends messages between your brain and other parts of your body

retina (RET-uhn-uh)—the lining inside the back of the eyeball

sign language (SINE LANG-gwij)—hand signs that stand for words, letters, and numbers

umami (oo-MAH-mee)—a savory taste found in meat and cheese

vibrate (VYE-brate)—to move back and forth rapidly

Read More

Garcia, Gabi. *Listening to My Body*. Austin, TX: Skinned Knee Publishing, 2019.

Murray, Julie. *The Five Senses*. Minneapolis: Abdo, 2016.

Owen, Ruth. *My Senses*. Minneapolis: Lerner Publications, 2017.

Internet Sites

DK Find Out: Taste
https://www.dkfindout.com/us/human-body/senses/taste

KidsHealth: All About Your Senses: Fun Experiments to Try
https://kidshealth.org/en/kids/experiment-main.html

Science Kids: Fun Senses Facts for Kids
http://www.sciencekids.co.nz/sciencefacts/humanbody/senses.html

Index